The Adventures of Tyler Brown Bear

And

The Long Vacation

I0101802

By Eloise E Kraemer

Haumea Publishing

First Edition

The Adventures of Tyler Brown Bear

The Long Vacation

Haumea Publishing Co.

First Edition

Printed by CreateSpace, Charleston, S.C., USA

ISBN: 978-0692551851

Introduction

Tyler Brown Bear, Rudy R. Hummingbird, Oscar T. Otter, Ted Turkey, the twin fawns, and many other young forest friends live in the Big Pine Forest, near the Great Meadow, in the mountains of North River, Idaho.

They are young and growing, not much different from children, like you, living in nearby towns and cities.

They also have families and friends, go to school, and learn life's lessons.

Just like all children, they find ways to have fun along the way.

Chapter 1 - A New Friend

Tyler B. Bear lived with Mother and Father Bear in a large pine tree forest in the mountains of North River, Idaho.

One spring morning, while Tyler was having his breakfast of milk and honeycombs, Mother Bear came in with her hat and coat on. A large basket was in her hand.

"Your father and I are going to get apples today from farmer Green's old root cellar. The cellar is by the red barn over the hill and across the big river."

"Now, be a good boy and don't wander too far from home. Don't talk to strangers."

"We should only be gone a short time."

 Mother and Father Bear waved, as they disappeared down a crooked trail that led over the hill.

Tyler Bear sat in his little red rocker, reading a book. The house was quiet. He could hear the clock on the wall tick-ticking away the seconds.

Tyler decided that maybe it would be better to go out to the back yard.

He put on his little blue jacket. He lifted his little green backpack onto his shoulders, just in case he found something for one of his many collections.

Tyler had many collections. He had rock collections, leaf collections, stick collections, and pine cone collections.

He had string collections, marble collections and feather collections.

His favorite collection of all was his feather collection. He had black feathers from Bob Crow, brown feathers from Oliver Owl, white feathers from Evie Eagle, blue feathers from Danny Heron, and a very large black and white feather from Clara Canadian Goose.

Tyler whistled a little tune as he walked through the giant pines, looking for something special for one of his collections.

Katie the chipmunk was busy gathering nuts and berries.

Ted Turkey and his sisters and brothers were hunting bugs under an old log.

"Do you want to go over to the old hollow tree and see if we can find any ants, or look for some new pinecones for my collection?" asked Tyler.

"I'm Sorry, Tyler. I am grounded. I got in trouble last night for practicing my low flying routine," replied Ted Turkey, looking not so happy.

Ted Turkey continued his story, "I knocked Mr. and Mrs. Squirrel's nest right out of the fork of the old maple tree!"

"It was a very lucky thing that the squirrel family was out to dinner over at the fairgrounds. Mother and Father are helping them fix their nest right now."

Tyler was sorry for Ted Turkey, but happy the squirrel family was not hurt.

"I'm sorry, Ted, I guess I'll be seeing you in school next week," replied Tyler.

Tyler walked on down the path.

He decided to see if there were any fresh wild strawberries growing by the edge of the meadow.

Mother bear had said, "Stay out of the meadow."

Rowdy Dog, Farmer Green's old hound dog loved to dig in the big meadow. Rowdy also loved to chase the woodland animals.

The strawberries were at the *edge* of the meadow, so Tyler decided it was probably okay.

When Tyler got to the edge of the meadow, he saw that Cheyenne and Sophia, twin whitetail fawns, were already busily eating on the strawberries. They offered to share a few of the strawberries with him in the shade of a large birch tree that stood at the edge of the meadow.

The day was warm. The buzzing sounds of the bee family gathering their daily honey from the meadow flowers and the gurgling of a nearby brook soon put Tyler Bear and the twin fawns to sleep.

Tyler awoke to find he was alone under the tree. The twin fawns had wandered off to find their mother.

Just then, Tyler Bear heard a small high pitched chirping coming from a nearby rose bush, and what sounded like some rustling and tussling.

Tyler crept quietly over to the bush. He spied a beautiful gray-green feather lying beside the bush. Who had left such a nice feather for his collection? He held the feather up to the sun. It shone brightly like the waves in McKinsey Lake on a sunny day.

Then, Tyler heard the rustling sound in the bushes again. He cautiously peered into the bush. There, upside down, stuck on one of the rose thorns, was the tiniest bird Tyler B. Bear had ever seen!

The little bird had a grayish colored head and body with a light dusting of rusty brown on the edges of his chest and back. There were a number of very tiny dark spots, like freckles on his chest. Across his neck and back, like Batman's cape, were soft feathers that shone like a green light. His sharp little beak and soft tail were tipped with a fine line of black.

This was the owner of the new feather Tyler Bear had found!

"What are you doing in there?" asked Tyler Bear.

"Hanging upside down!" replied the baby bird.

"Why would you want to do that?" asked Tyler.

"I am stuck!"

"Please help me get out of here!" replied the baby bird.

"Well, just be still, and I'll see what I can do." replied Tyler Bear, scratching his head, trying to figure out how to get the baby out without getting caught in the bush himself.

Gently, he poked a stick toward the branch holding the baby bird. He ever so softly pushed the branch back. The baby bird dropped onto a soft pink rose just below the sticky branch above.

The tiny bird sat there a moment, then his wings started buzzing like a honey bee.

ZIP! Out he flew, like a flash, and up into the old birch tree.

Then, back down he flew, zippity zip, sticking his longish little beak into the depths of another large pink rose on the edge of the bush.

After a moment of slurp, slurping, drinking the sweet honey inside of the rose, the baby bird perched on the side of a nearby log and spoke.

"Hello there! My name is Rudy. Rudy Rufous Hummingbird. What's yours?"

For a moment, Tyler was too shocked to speak. Then, he cleared his throat. It felt like he had a strawberry still stuck inside his throat, or something.

"Hello there. My name is Tyler B. Bear, and I live in the Big Pine Forest. It is good to meet you."

Tyler Bear discovered that Rudy Hummingbird was quite friendly and liked to tell jokes.

Rudy asked Tyler Bear, "What happens when a songbird loses his voice?"

Tyler had no idea.

"I don't know, Rudy, what does happen?"

Rudy answered, with a little giggle, "He becomes a HUMMINGBIRD, get it?"

Tyler thought that was so funny, he rolled in the grass laughing.

Tyler asked Rudy, "What type of comb does a bear like?"

Rudy looked confused. "I don't know!"

"They like a honeycomb!" Tyler laughed.

Rudy shook his head. I think I make better jokes than you do!

They played hide and seek. Rudy was small enough to hide behind branches and leaves, but his buzzing gave him away.

Tyler Bear crouched behind bushes and behind rocks, but he

was so big, his tail or his ears usually stuck out, giving him away.

The sun was getting low in the sky. It was time to head home.

Tyler said good-by to Rudy R. Hummingbird at Rudy's home in the tall birch tree, at the edge of the meadow and started off for his home in the pine forest.

Chapter 2 - Apple Pie and Guests

When Tyler Bear got home, Mother and Father Bear were already there. A basket of large red apples was sitting in the kitchen. Father Bear was dozing in his chair.

Mother Bear was slicing apples for an apple pie.

"Your father caught some nice fresh fish at the big North River," explained Mother Bear.

"Dinner will be ready in a moment."

"Hurry and wash up"

"Yummy! Fresh fish and apple pie! What more could a little bear want!" thought Tyler B. Bear.

Tyler bear went to sleep that night with a very full tummy and a head full of dreams about playing with his newly found friend, Rudy R. Hummingbird.

The next morning, Tyler slept in.

When he awoke, Father Bear was already fixing a broken chair while Mother Bear sewed on a new pair of blue pants for him.

Tyler was growing fast, as were all the young animals of the forest. Tyler had already outgrown many of his clothes that Mother Bear had made for him in the spring.

Tyler was just finishing up his breakfast when there came a knock at the door.

Mother Bear opened the door to find Mr. and Mrs. Hoot Owl standing on the porch.

"Why, Mr. and Mrs. Hoot Owl, how are you doing this fine morning?" asked Mother Bear.

"We are quite fine, thank you." Mr. Owl responded, placing some glasses on eyes that were big and round.

"We are making the rounds of the forest neighborhood, creating a list of all the forest children that will be attending school this year."

School for forest animal children was different than school was for children in town. School in the forest ran from May through September.

Mrs. Bear invited the Owl's in and served them some mint tea.

"School will be held down by the old pond near the big stump that stands near rocky ridge," explained Mr. Owl, in a very serious voice.

"All children must bring a lunch and be prepared to be on their best behavior."

"We have more children in class this year. Many new residents have moved into the neighborhood since the big fire in hickory hollow last fall," continued Mr. Owl.

"I am sure that you won't have any trouble from our Tyler," said Mother Bear.

"Tyler knows his manners and is a good little bear."

"He will be there on time, Monday morning."

The Owls thanked Mr. and Mrs. Bear for the tea and left with a flutter.

Chapter 3 - A Muddy Mistake

Monday morning, Tyler B. Bear was awakened to the sound of Mr. and Mrs. Robin singing a new song. They were announcing the hatch of three new children.

Mother Bear was making breakfast in the kitchen.

"Hurry, Tyler and get dressed. Your new blue pants are hanging over the chair. Don't forget to bush your fur. You want to look nice for school."

Tyler stretched and yawned. He didn't really feel like school today. He wanted to play in the big meadow with his new friend, Rudy R. Hummingbird.

He slowly put on his new blue pants and brushed out his soft brown fur. He washed his face and hands and ate his breakfast.

Mother bear gave him a lunch of apples and honeycomb, kissed him on the head and sent him off to school.

Tyler grunted as he walked down the path to school.

"I don't think school should start on a sunny day. I think a sunny day is meant for little bears to play!"

When he got to school, he saw his friends, Rudy Hummingbird and Oscar Otter. Oscar was trying to teach Rudy how to slide down the mud slide by the side of the old pond using an oak leaf as a sled. Rudy was having a problem hanging on as the oak leaf sled hit a rough spot on the muddy bank of the pond.

"Let me give it a try!" shouted Tyler.

"Here, Rudy, climb into my ear and hang onto my fur and I'll slide on my rear!"

Down the slide they went. **Swish! Bump!** Slipppperrrrty, **SPASH!**

They went so fast down the muddy slide, they flew into the water of the old pond at the bottom! Muddy water splashed up all over Mr. Owl as he approached the group of children by the side of the old pond.

"WHOs idea was this?" demanded Mr. Owl.

"Mine…." replied Tyler Bear, looking like a very wet little bear, indeed.

Rudy Rufous Hummingbird was busy buzzing around in circles, trying to dry his feathers from his trip into the pond.

"You will see me after school, Tyler Bear!" hooted Mr. Owl.

"Now, all you children, please be seated on the old log and we will begin our lessons."

With that, Mr. Owl fluffed out his feathers and proceeded to give the forest children lessons.

The lessons included subjects like "Eating the Right Foods", "The Three Dangers of the Forest, (fire, flood, and man)", and "The History of Hide and Seek".

Chapter 4 – A Visit With Mr. Owl

After school, Tyler went up to Mr. Owl's perch in the old oak tree.

Mr. Owl was busy studying a worm crawling up the trunk of the tree. He blinked as Tyler announced his presence.

"Here I am, Mr. Owl. I am very sorry to have disrupted class this morning. I didn't mean to get you wet."

"Well, Tyler Bear, the next time you decide to take a trip down the muddy slide, please be sure you watch out for those around you when you make a big SPLASH!"

"Here is your punishment. On your way home today, you need to engage your mind and not your mouth. You need to find two things that live, but do not move."

"Report back to me, tomorrow, what you find. Now, off with you, before your parents worry."

Tyler headed for home, thinking about his chore. "What is alive, but does not move?"

"Is a rock alive? No, a rock does not breathe. It does not eat. A rock is not alive."

"What about a tree? Yes, a tree is alive, but it stands in one place. Does a tree move?"

Just then, the wind blew the branches of the tree. The branches reached for Tyler Bear's ear and caught on his fur.

"Oh yes, the wind moves the tree. Its branches can sway and reach in the wind. A tree can move."

Little Tyler Bear walked on. He spied a white mushroom at the side of the path.

"What about a mushroom? Yes! A mushroom is a plant. It is alive, yet, it cannot move to another spot. The wind cannot move it. A mushroom is alive but cannot move."

*The mushroom could be number ONE."

"What about the old log? No, the old log is no longer alive."

Tyler Bear stepped upon a piece of soft moss by a large rock. The moss was cool and soft under his tired little feet.

"I got it! Moss! Moss is alive. It is a plant, but it does not move. It has to sit all day in the same spot.

When the rain falls and the wind blows, it cannot move to shelter. "

"Moss can be my number TWO!"

Tyler Bear was happy once again as he headed home from his first day at school.

He couldn't wait to impress Mr. Hoot Owl the next day at school.

Chapter 5 – The Lesson

When Tyler Bear finally arrived home, that evening, his troubles were not over.

"What have you done to your new blue pants, Tyler Brown Bear?" his mother scolded."

"No blackberry pie for you, young man!"

Tyler was not a happy little bear when he went to bed that night. There was a vacant place in his tummy where that blackberry pie should have been.

"I suppose I had better remember to put on my old pants next time I decide to go sliding on the muddy slide beside the pond!" thought Tyler Bear.

"Maybe, I should not make such a big splash either."

The next day, Tyler was the first student to be seated for lessons on the big old log by the pond.

Mr. Owl fluttered down right in front of Tyler Bear.

"Well, Tyler Bear, I see you are here promptly this morning. Did you complete your assignment?"

"Yes, sir," announced Tyler Bear.

"I certainly did!"

"I found two things on my way home that are alive and do not ever move!"

"What might those two things be?" inquired Mr. Hoot Owl.

"A mushroom and moss," replied Tyler Bear.

"I am sorry. You are mistaken," replied Mr. Owl.

"Everything that lives must move."

"Some things may not appear to move, but everything that lives must grow. You must move to grow!"

Little Tyler Bear thought about that for a while.

Mr. Hoot Owl was right. Even the tiny moss grew.

"I guess that is why Mr. Hoot Owl is our teacher," thought Tyler B. Bear.

"He knows more than we do."

Chapter 6 - Summer Days

Spring turned into summer. Tyler Bear and Rudy Hummingbird became the very best of friends. Every day after school they played in the forest and the great meadow.

Tyler helped himself to honey from the honey bee tree while Rudy sipped honey from the nearby honeysuckle vines.

On warm summer days, they played in the old birch tree by the side of the big meadow.

Tyler would swing from the big branches of the old birch, pretending he was a **VERY** large bird.

Rudy would sit on a tiny branch by his little bird home and pretend he was **VERY** a small bear.

When the weather was very warm, they visited Oscar Otter and his family by the side of the old pond.

They learned to slide together on the muddy slippery slide. They still got a bit muddy, but, Tyler Bear was very careful to make sure he wore his old pants and learned not to make **TOO** big of a splash!

Tyler Bear, Rudy R. Hummingbird, and all of the forest children worked very hard to be good at hide and seek.

It was important to be good at hide and seek just in case hunters came into the forest.

There were many types of hunters.

There was Old Mr. Cougar, who liked young rabbit, bird or a little bear for dinner.

There was Rowdy Dog, Farmer Green's hound, who loved to chase rabbits, mice, birds, deer and little bears, just for sport.

There was Farmer Green who, it is said, has a nice large stew pot he likes to fill with little animals from the forest.

Chapter 7 – The Very Long Nap

As the autumn winds blew through the great meadow, the forest children flew kites made from the leaves of the great oak tree.

They bounced and played in huge piles of leaves colored red, orange, yellow and brown. The leaves formed huge soft mounds as they fell under the forest trees.

Tyler Bear, Ted Turkey and his sister, Lucy, Rudy R.

Hummingbird and Oscar Otter, splashed and played in the pools of water made from the autumn rains.

One fall day, Tyler Bear woke to a new feeling in the air. The air was much cooler.

Mother Bear had Tyler put on his new woolen coat before he went outdoors. There was a dusting of white over the ground and trees that looked like sugar. The white dusting tasted like cold water as it melted in Tyler's mouth.

"What is this?" Tyler asked Mother Bear.

"It is called snow."

"It comes with winter," replied Mother Bear.

Little Tyler Bear decided to find his friend, Rudy Hummingbird. It would be fun to play in the snow together. Maybe they could go down to the pond and slide on the snow with the otters.

Tyler Bear set off for Rudy Hummingbird's home in the old birch tree.

When Tyler arrived at Rudy R. Hummingbird's tree house, he found no one at home. Hanging on the door was a sign that read, "See you in the spring!"

Tyler was confused. What had happened to his friend? Where did his family go? Why did they leave?

His head drooped as he headed back home to Mother Bear.

"I have lost my friend!" exclaimed Tyler B. Bear, holding back his tears.

"Mother, the Hummingbird family is gone! Where did they go?"

"Why would they leave? I don't understand!"

"Don't worry, dear," Mother Bear consoled.

"They will only be gone for a while."

"They went on vacation to Mexico for the winter."

"Mexico is a country far south of the Big Pine Forest. It is in Central America. It will be warm there when the winter winds blow through the Big Pine Forest of North River, Idaho."

"Your friend, Rudy, and his family are probably on the beach in Mexico right now, enjoying the warm sun."

"Don't worry, though. Winter will be over in the blink of an eye."

"Springtime will follow, and your friend and his family will return when the spring flowers start to bloom."

"Now, wipe your eyes and have some nice ant porridge and honeycomb."

"I am going to give you a good bath before you settle down for your long winter nap."

After a nice bowl of porridge and a warm bath, Mother Bear tucked Tyler Brown Bear into his little bed for a very long winter nap.

Mother and Father Bear set their alarm clock for "spring". They donned their night clothes and settled down in their very large feather bed for their long winter nap.

Chapter 8 – A New Year

When Tyler Bear awoke from his long winter nap, the winter snows were gone. The birds were singing. The bright springtime sun was shining. The trees were blossoming, and the bees were buzzing.

Tyler climbed out of his bed. It looked much smaller than when he had got into it for his winter nap!

He reached for his little blue britches. He put his foot in the first leg.

It got stuck! He could not pull on his little blue britches!

Tyler Bear had grown during his long winter nap!

His mother came in with brand new red britches with shiny new buttons on them and larger pockets for collecting.

Tyler went to sit in his little red rocking chair.

Oh, My! The red rocking chair was so much smaller than he remembered!

It was too small for him to sit in.

Father bear came in with a brand new middle-sized bright yellow rocking chair that fit Tyler Bear in all the right places!

The whole Bear Family was very hungry that morning.

Father Bear had gone down to the big North River and caught six shiny trout.

Mother Bear had picked a nice basket of fresh blackberries.

Tyler ate a very, very large breakfast, that morning, of blackberries and trout. He even had a second helping of everything.

Then, Tyler Bear announced that he was going out to play.

"Don't be gone too long, Tyler B. Bear," warned Mother Bear.

"Mr. and Mrs. Owl will be coming by today."

"We need to get you enrolled in school. They will be surprised to see how you have grown!"

Tyler Bear picked up his little green backpack to put it on.

The straps would not fit over his now larger shoulders! The

backpack seemed to be much, **MUCH** smaller.

Mother Bear gave him a new, red backpack with bright new buckles. He put it on. It fit just right!

Tyler started out down the path towards Rudy Hummingbird's home.

Around a bend in the path, Keira Cottontail was chasing a butterfly.

"Good Morning, Tyler Bear!" shouted Keira.

"Do you want to chase butterflies with me?".

"That would be fun, Keira," said Tyler, "but I have to see if my friend, Rudy is back from Mexico."

Tyler Bear walked on.

When Tyler reached the old pond, he saw Ted Turkey and his sister, Lucy Turkey, nearby, looking for bugs under the old log.

"Hi there, Tyler Brown Bear!" shouted Ted Turkey.

"Come on down and have some bugs with us!"

"There are plenty of nice fat ants to go around!"

"Nice to see you too, Tom," replied Tyler.

"Sorry, I have to be on my way. I am headed to the old birch tree by the big meadow to see if Rudy Hummingbird has returned from his vacation."

With that, Tyler hurried on down the path

Just as Tyler Bear reached the far end of the old pond, Oscar Otter's head popped up out of the water.

"Where are you going in such a hurry, Tyler Brown Bear?" Oscar asked.

"Oh, I'm on my way to the old birch tree to see if the Hummingbird Family has returned from Mexico yet," replied Tyler.

"Well, just watch out for Rowdy, Farmer Green's big brown hound dog. He has been snooping about down by the meadow today."

Oscar continued, "Mr. and Mrs. Field Mouse and their six children just scurried by here, saying that they barely escaped with their tails."

"I guess Rowdy Hound Dog has been digging holes all over the Meadow in search of mice and rabbits."

Tyler Bear was not too excited about the prospect of meeting Farmer Green's big brown dog, Rowdy.

Tyler's cousin, Christopher Bear, had his new red overalls torn in a close call with Rowdy Hound Dog just last spring.

It seems that Christopher was fishing in the old pond when Rowdy happened by.

Rowdy Hound Dog chased poor Christopher Bear up a pine tree, where Christopher sat, pitifully, howling away, while Rowdy barked, underneath.

Luckily, Auntie Madelyn Bear heard Christopher's howls and arrived on the scene just in time. She chased Rowdy Dog home with his tail between his legs!

Chapter 9 – The Meeting

Tyler Bear was just thinking of how funny it would have been to see Rowdy Dog running away with his tail between his legs, when he heard a snuffing sound behind a bush beside the old birch tree where Rudy lived.

Before Tyler could scurry for shelter, Rowdy Dog pounced out from behind the bush.

Tyler bear let out a howl. Rowdy Dog let out a series of bark, bark, barks. The chase was on.

Tyler probably could have outrun Rowdy Dog, who was just as surprised as Tyler at the meeting, if Tyler had not, at that moment, stumbled into one of the holes Rowdy Dog had dug.

Bump, boom, down he went! Tyler Bear rolled down a small hill and bumped into a rock at the bottom.

"**Bark, bark, bark**," Rowdy Hound Dog came, running, ears flapping, tail straight out.

"Oh, no!" thought Tyler, "This is the end!"

Chapter 10 – A Friend Indeed

All of a sudden, Tyler heard a very loud buzzing right by his head. Zip, zippity zip, a hummingbird, not quite as tiny, but still quite small, flew around his head. It was Rudy!

Rudy Rufous Hummingbird wore bright new feathers. Under his throat, he sported a smart yellow and rusty orange bow-tie. He had a nice little greenish brown coat with a brown and white vest.

His new green wing feathers with black tips beat like a fan at high speed.

Then, Rudy dove down, down, down.

ZIP, zippity, zip!

He dove down, right straight for Rowdy Dog's big black nose.

Buzz, buzz ,buzz,

Rudy R. Hummingbird then began to peck Rowdy Hound Dog right on the end of his nose.

"Yelp!" Rowdy Dog turned and ran as fast as his legs would carry him toward Farmer Green's farmhouse.

Tyler B, Bear and Rudy R. Hummingbird laughed at the sight until their tummies ached.

"Hello Tyler!" shouted Rudy Rufous Hummingbird.

"I guess I got back from vacation just in time!"

Tyler got up and dusted his pants off.

"Wow! That was a close one!"

"It's sure great to see you, Rudy R. Hummingbird!"

"Are you ready to have some more fun?"

With that, they raced off to the Big Pine Forest to find some more of their forest friends.

www.ingramcontent.com/pod-product-compliance
Lightning Source LLC
Chambersburg PA
CBHW060635280326
41933CB00012B/2043